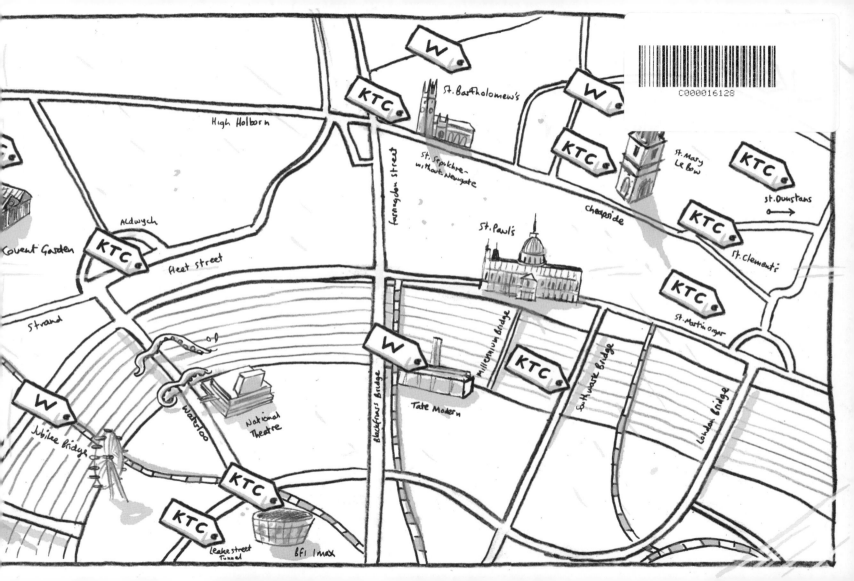

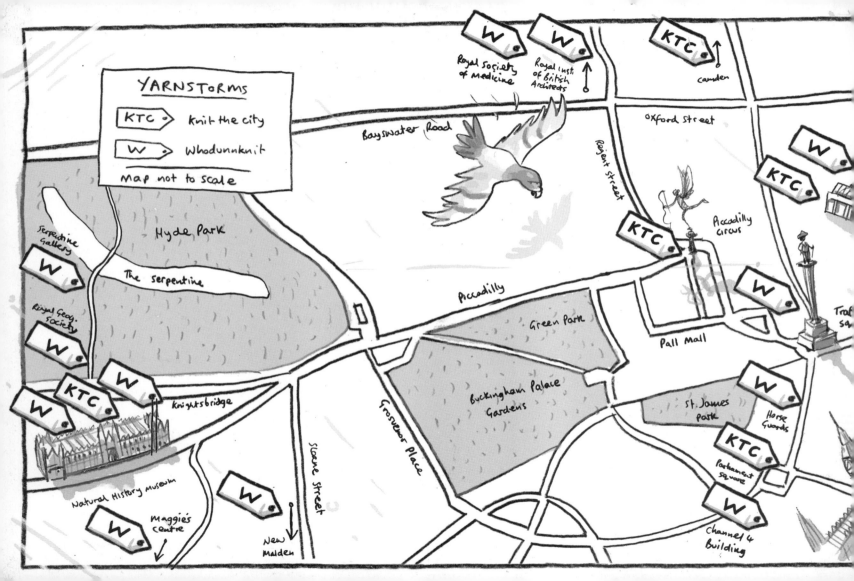

KNIT THE CITY
a whodunnknit set in london

Deadly Knitshade

summersdale

KNIT THE CITY

This edition published in 2011 by Summersdale Publishers Ltd.

First published in Germany © by Hoffmann und Campe Verlag, Hamburg in 2011

Map by Gary Northfield

All images for Stitched Sea Life Escapees used courtesy of London's Natural History Museum

Summersdale Publishers Ltd
46 West Street
Chichester
West Sussex
PO19 1RP
UK

www.summersdale.com

Printed and bound in China

ISBN: 978-1-84953-179-5

Substantial discounts on bulk quantities of Summersdale books are available to corporations, professional associations and other organisations. For details contact Summersdale Publishers by telephone: +44 (0) 1243 771107, fax: +44 (0) 1243 786300 or email: nicky@summersdale.com.

For my dad who said I would

For my mum and Neh who said I should

and for my Sheepsketcher who knew I could

CONTENTS

THE STORY

The Gathering of Knit the City

Once upon a time there was a city. A city of so many stories that they ran through its streets and slid down its rooftops like rainwater. A city that lived and breathed and created its histories all day and all night with each beat of its story-soft heart.

Some stories grew longer, and larger, and louder than the rest. The tendrils of their tales wrapped around and around; self-important, shiny, selfish and new. Each morning the city's people poured from its homes to form a many-legged and many-wheeled beast; belching money, smoke and all things modern.

The beast hurried and harried, then huffed and went home. It rarely saw more than the pavement before its smart-shoed feet, as its story stomped and stamped across the city's streets.

In the wake of this beast, the beat of the city's story-soft heart grew more and more quiet. The colourless concrete, cold and cheerless, sprang up on all sides. The beat grew so faint that if you stopped to listen for its rhythm you could barely hear it. But people rarely stopped to listen and they rarely stopped to look.

All was not lost, though. One day a sneaky stitcher stepped outside the stampede to sit, and to knit, and to stitch herself a story. Under the 'click, clack, click' of her needles she heard the heartbeat, she sensed the city's shiver, and a yarn-flavoured storm started to brew.

Deadly Knitshade stalked the depths of the London Underground, a pair of knitting needles in her hands, an army of twitch-whiskered Tube mice at her feet and her knitblasts at her fingertips.

Eyeing the commuter beast that stomped and stamped on smaller stories, she decided to take a stitched stand.

Her woolly whisper crept out into the dark streets and deep shadows of the stitching world and beckoned kindred spirits of the needle and hook. From the darkest corner of the library amongst bookworms and bindings rustled the Bluestocking Stitcher, in a cloud of curse words and degenerate butterflies.

From the green and rolling country hills galloped Lady Loop, the secretly siphoned fleeces of the gentry's sheep tucked safe in her saddlebags.

From the vampire-haunted ballrooms of Vienna waltzed the Purple Purler, a distant cousin of the Scarlet Pimpernel, flourishing a hook and leaving crocheted calling cards.

From the ovine-cropped grasses of Wales and New Zealand shuffled Shorn-a the Dead, a strange sheep-dip smile on her lips and a thread-snipping shuriken about her neck.

From the far-east mountaintops leapt the silent Knitting Ninja, a whirl of wild wool, cherry blossom and crafty kung fu.

And from behind the silver screen crept the quick-fingered Fastener, all buttons and bows and unending misbehaviour.

The campaign of wool and whispers had begun.

The Birth of the Yarnstorm

Knit the City was born of hands not content to lounge idly on the arms of living room sofas; of a rhythm of stitch after stitch that slowed the daily whirlwind to an easy amble; and a bone-aching passion for a city each sneaky stitcher had fallen in love with. Seven threads of stitching stories that tangled with those of the streets.

My first solo 'knitblast', a moment when the knitting I have created and the space I am sat in suddenly snap together, took place before the disapproving eyes of the quite frankly terrifying blue whale in London's Natural History Museum.

It was not a case of 'look at me' or 'look what I made'. It was a stitched squeal of delight, a knitted tug at the sleeve or squeeze of the hand of those who visited after me. A breathless wool-based whisper of 'Look where we are! Isn't this place jaw-droppingly amazing?' and really nothing more.

When winter hit London and washed the streets in wind, the Knit the City Yarn Corps was officially formed. Six sneaky stitchers (with a seventh agent joining later) who crafted for all kinds of reasons, but whose love of craft and passion for the city's stories tied them together. In a secret wool-lined bunker in an undisclosed location, we sat and planned our first fibre-based foray: a combined series of Yarn Corps knitblasts that would end, often unexpectedly, in something knittedly beautiful and scarily easy to love. London became our concrete and steel canvas.

Amongst the tourist tangle of Covent Garden, we cosied a wooden barrier. Returning hours later we caught a group of French tourists standing about it and stroking it as if it suddenly lived and breathed under its woolly pelt. It was a fine fibre-flavoured beginning but it left us unfulfilled. The city demanded more.

In the CCTV-infested Parliament Square, where protesters are moved along by world-weary police officers, we covered a public telephone box in knitting. As we clothed the call box, two police officers appeared. The bad cop handed us a 'Stop and Search' notice, perturbed to find no box to tick to file a phone box cosy into its law-abiding niche. The good cop smiled from under his peaked cap and took a photo on his phone 'For the wife, who likes a bit of knitting'.

As the phone box stood in its new woolly jacket the city around it changed. Tired office workers broke into the smiles they reserved only for weekends. They stopped to throw their arms around the cosy communication cubicle, like the tree-hugging hippies that we all are deep down. Tourists slowed to snap, smile and take home a story.

Later from the safety of a nearby pub we listened to the city. Not bad, it seemed to say, but I know you can do better. So to the Leake Street Tunnel, under the wheel-screams and commuter scurry of Waterloo Station. A place where the air is wheezy with spray-can art as graffiti artists from all over lend their layer to the

once-Banksied walls, without having to worry about the long arm of the law. A legal graffiti area since 2008, it lacks the heart-squeezing rush of forbidden art, but makes up for it with less panicked swirls of colour as artists find their freedom in the great outdoors.

Our Leake Street 'Web of Woe' dragged craft into artists' territory, as I narrowed my eyes at our chosen space and saw the tendrils of tales sprouting from the walls. There in the warm underbelly of Waterloo Station, we trapped 44 horrified handmade creatures in the web of a fat-yet-famished Knit the City spider. A full 13 feet from end to end, our web twitched with the death throes of insects, myths, lost romances, rodents, dust sprites, and foul-mouthed butterflies that you would not take home to your kids.

We were no longer simply 'covering objects in knitting'. The city's stories were winding their way through our work. Our stitched squeals of city delight now had the city speaking through them, and the Knit the City Yarnstorm was born.

Knit the World

Knit the City is not limited to the London we can reach out and wrap yarn around. It is also about the London that glows from screens around the globe.

We were the first, and only, yarnstorming collective to drag the online world with us on every adventure. We tweeted the first ever live London yarnstorm on Twitter; inviting followers to virtually stalk us on our Oranges and Lemons Odyssey.

Our city stories spoke to distant watchers who may never enjoy fish, chips and mushy peas with plenty of salt and vinegar, or get tutted at by fellow train travellers when their Oyster card fails to work first time and they get stuck at the Underground ticket barriers. Our blog-posted yarnstorms guided strangers through a virtual London in a way a mere postcard picture might struggle to get across.

We interrupt this live yarnstorm to have lunch. We suggest you eat too.

2:23 PM August via iPhone

Wikipedia states that 'yarn bombing is almost exclusively about beautification and creativity'. We're hoping to add a line or two to that. Knit the City doesn't seek to change the world; to stop the wars, egg the prime minister, mop up oil spills, or ratchet up the trendiness of the over-60s and their skills (though there isn't a knitting granny we don't take our handmade hats off to).

It is true that we yarnstorm because it is just so much fun. London tempts us in with its long-forgotten sagas, its rarely glimpsed corners of charm and chatter, and its twists of tradition. We can't help but take our stitching and go when we're called, and can't help but drag the unsuspecting London commuter beast with us. We take it warmly by its sweaty hands and worry it with our needles until it stands still, takes its head out of the newspaper and looks up.

You'll most likely be surprised to know that the world is riddled with secret stashes of yarnstorming groups. There are crews worldwide from America's 'Knitta Please', to Canada's 'Yarmbombing', to Australia's 'Grrl + Dogg', to Holland's 'Knitted Landscape' (whose 'Banksy' rat you can see on the right) and the German countryside's Molli Woodtagger to name but a few. We can't claim to be pioneers of the public purl. We can't claim to be the first to battle the blinkered commuter beast. The idea that we're 'artists subverting the world's view of traditional craft' has, on occasion, made us laugh till we've dropped stitches.

But as we relax in the secret safety of the wool-lined Knit the City bunker, sharpening our needles, sipping pear cider and planning woolly city-wide trails of tales, we realise something important. We'd do it even if none of you were watching. The city's story-soft heart beats on beneath our stitches and that is enough.

So I invite you to wander through the woolly worlds of Whodunnknit and Knit the City.

Take your time, slow your pace and let the 'click, clack, click' of our needles and hooks tell you stitched stories of horror, heroes and handmade happy ever after.

Enjoy the yarnstormed show.

Deadly Knitshade

WHODUNNKNITS

Deadly Knitshade's fledging fibre-flung solo 'Whodunnknits' were looped to life as simple stripy socks. Socks that began life as 'knit, knit, knit' and 'purl, purl, purl', and ended up waving woolly appendages in the smoggy London outdoors.

On her double-decker charger, armed with Oyster travel card, trusty Swiss Army knife and a bagful of hand-knitted nefariousness, the sneaky stitcher went trip-trap trip-trap around the city, leaving wonder and wool in her wake.

13

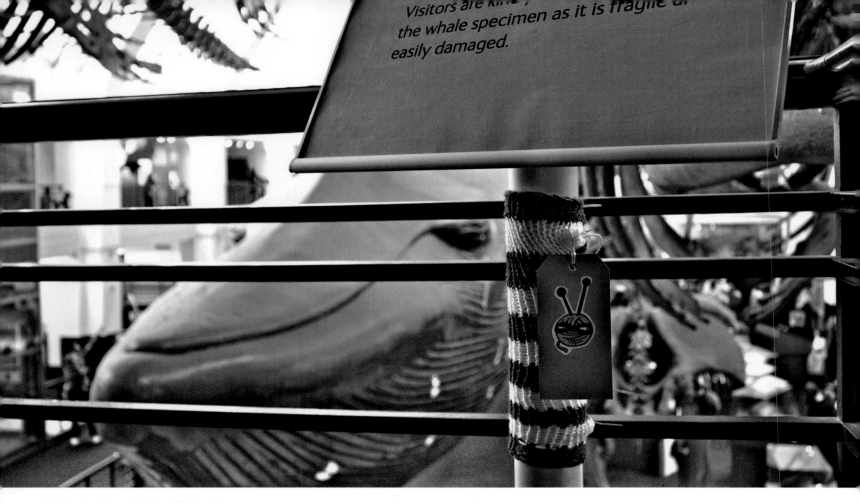

Visitors are ki~~ ~~
the whale specimen as it is fragile ~~ ~~
easily damaged.

A Woolly Wave in the Whale Room:
Old Blue-fins is deeply unimpressed

St Bartholomews Cosy Phonecord:
'I just purled to say I love you'

Signpost Stitchery in Covent Garden:
Knitshade Blues

Floral Zebra Leg in Tate Modern:

The melancholy tale of a badly crocheted flower

Punk Polecover in Trafalgar Square:

While Nelson isn't looking

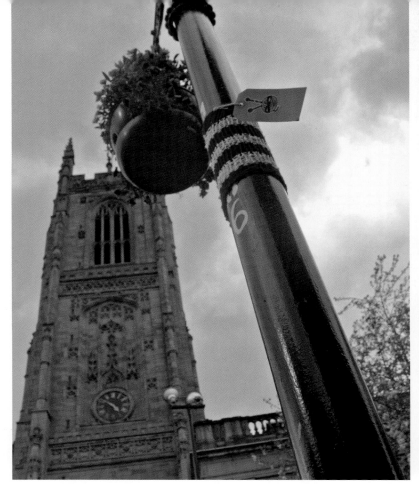

Holy Knitted Lamp Post Cosy, Batman at Derby Cathedral:
Purple and purled

On Yer Bike:
A station-side cycle gets knitted

What happens to abandoned graffiti knitting?

Pink Furry Knitting: So we're going sightseeing, eh? Yay! How exciting! In Central London!

Deadly Knitshade: Yup. Central London. I'll take you to see the London Eye if you like.

PFK: Really? The London Eye? Wow! Gosh! That's ever-so-nice of you.

DK: Ah, don't mention it.

PFK: And… you won't leave me there, will you?

DK: What do you mean?

PFK: Well, I sort of noticed that when you've taken some of my woolly siblings out. Well, they... *lowers voice* … haven't come home.

DK: I told you where they were. Didn't I?

PFK (mumbling): You said they got stolen by pigeons.

DK: What was that? Speak up. What did I tell you?

PFK (louder): They got stolen by pigeons.

DK: Exactly. But you don't have to worry. I spent hours making you. I wouldn't just abandon you and let a pigeon steal you. Now would I? Hmm? *tickles knitting under chin* Hmm?

PFK (giggling): Hee hee. No. Of course not. Silly, silly me…

Later:

PFK: Hello? Hello...?

sound of pigeon wings flapping and clawed feet landing on the railing of Millennium Bridge

darkness

WEB OF WOE

Beneath the busy city, underneath the non-stop hurry-scurry of London's Waterloo Station was a damp and sun-shy tunnel of graffiti wonders. Here the hungry Knit the City spider sat and spun his web of woe. A full 13 feet from end to sticky stitched end the web spelled a woolly demise for all 44 of its handmade victims. A yarnstorm not for the faint of heart.

Freedom pleas
eloquently croaked and
slightly less polite...

... the last lamenting wingbeats of handmade Mothra...

... from the sticky prison came the squeaks and squeals of spider food...

... daring rescues and
bug-eyed horror...

... legends, leavers...

... and long-faced
losers...

... thousand-yard stares...

... famous last words...

... furry farewells and the empty-stomached rumble of one very hungry arachnid owner. Knit the City had created handmade horror. We were very proud indeed.

It is rumoured that the Spider sets one sticky victim free to tell the tale to those who may follow.
Beware the Web of Woe, friends, beware.

ORANGES AND LEMONS ODYSSEY

Once upon a time there were six lonely, grey and stony cold churches hidden in corners of a roaring smoke-filled city. These churches had proud histories, they had lived in the city for many years, and long ago someone had thought so much of them they had written them into a nursery rhyme and made their singing bells the stars.

But that was long ago; before the sirens, screeches and circus of the city drowned them out.

If you listen very carefully when you pass these churches you might hear their lonely bells whisper.

31

'Oranges and Lemons,' said the bells of St Clements.

'You owe me five farthings,' said the bells of St Martins.

'When will you pay me?' said the bells of Old Bailey.

'When I grow rich,' said the bells of Shoreditch.

'When will that be?' said the bells of Stepney.

'I do not know,' said the great bells of Bow.

WALL OF WONDERLAND

The Yarn Corps were beginning to get very tired of sitting on the South Bank, and of having nothing to do. They were considering (as well as they could, for the hot day made them feel very sleepy and stupid), whether the pleasure of knitting something sneaky would be worth the trouble of getting up and finding the yarn, when suddenly a white rabbit with pink eyes ran close by them.

Burning with curiosity, they ran across the pavement after it, and fortunately were just in time to see it pop down a large rabbit-hole under the hedge.

Down went the Yarn Corps after it, never once considering how in the world they were to get out again.

'Well!' thought Alice to herself, 'after such a fall as this, I shall think nothing of tumbling down stairs!'

'Oh my ears and whiskers, how late it's getting!'

'Are you content now?' said the Caterpillar.

'Well, I should like to be a LITTLE larger, sir, if you wouldn't mind,' said Alice: 'three inches is such a wretched height to be.'

'It is a very good height indeed!' said the Caterpillar angrily, rearing itself upright as it spoke (it was exactly three inches high).

Alice remained looking thoughtfully at the mushroom for a minute, trying to make out which were the two sides of it; and as it was perfectly round, she found this a very difficult question.

'Have you guessed the riddle yet?' the Hatter said, turning to Alice again.

'No, I give it up,' Alice replied: 'What's the answer?'

'I haven't the slightest idea,' said the Hatter.

'Have some wine,' the March Hare said in an encouraging tone. Alice looked all round the table, but there was nothing on it but tea.

'I don't see any wine,' she remarked.

'There isn't any,' said the March Hare.

The Dormouse slowly opened his eyes. 'I wasn't asleep,' he said in a hoarse, feeble voice: 'I heard every word you fellows were saying.'

'Who ARE you talking to?' said the King, going up to Alice, and looking at the Cat's head with great curiosity.

'It's a friend of mine – a Cheshire Cat,' said Alice: 'Allow me to introduce it.'

'I don't like the look of it at all,' said the King: 'However, it may kiss my hand if it likes.'

'I'd rather not,' the Cat remarked.

The Queen turned
crimson with fury, and,
after glaring at her for a
moment like a wild beast,
screamed 'Off with her
head! Off—'

'Nonsense!' said Alice,
very loudly and decidedly,
and the Queen was silent.

'We must have a bit of a fight, but I don't care about going on long,' said Tweedledum. 'What's the time now?'

Tweedledee looked at his watch, and said 'Half-past four.'

'Let's fight till six, and then have dinner,' said Tweedledum.

So they went up to the Mock Turtle, who looked at them with large eyes full of tears, but said nothing.

'I'm sure I'll take you with pleasure!' the Queen said. 'Two pence a week, and jam every other day.'

Alice couldn't help laughing, as she said, 'I don't want you to hire me – and I don't care for jam.'

'It's very good jam,' said the Queen.

'Oh, I've had such a curious dream!' said Alice, and she told her sister, as well as she could remember them, all these strange adventures of hers that you have just been reading about.

And when she had finished, her sister kissed her, and said, 'It WAS a curious dream, dear, certainly: but now run in to your tea; it's getting late.'

So Alice got up and ran off, thinking while she ran, as well she might...

... what a wonderful dream it had been.

LONG NIGHT OF
THE STITCHED SHEEP

The challenge: to complete the longest yarnstorm in the history of the city, while conquering the seemingly endless 20-mile London Night Hike. One long night. Twenty miles of London streets. Ten stitched sheep. Eight yarnstorm targets.

One very good cause. Two potentially very sore feet.

Stitched Sheep 1:
Guildhall. The Night Hike begins. Green is for Go Sheep.

Stitched Sheep 2:
Channel 4. Reality TV Karaoke Sheep.

Stitched Sheep 3:
Royal Geographical Society. Latin Learning Sheep.

Stitched Sheep 4:
Maggie's Cancer Caring Centre. How Can I Help You? Sheep.

Stitched Sheep 5: Maggie's Cancer Caring Centre. Lightly Scented Relaxation Sheep.

Stitched Sheep 6:
Serpentine Gallery. This is Not a Sheep Modern Art Sheep.

Stitched Sheep 7:
Royal Society of Medicine. Plucky Poloraid Sheep.

Stitched Sheep 8: Royal Institute of British Architects. Play It Again Sheep.

Stitched Sheep 9:
Horse Guards.
Paper Lantern Love Sheep.

Stitched Sheep 10:
Guildhall. Night Hike finish line.
Sit Down Before You Fall Down Triumph Sheep.

PLUNDER OF PIRATES

Shiver me stitched timbers! Here be pirates. Here be blasted bilge mice. Here be wenches. Here be hordes of scurvy pirate butterflies. Here be what too much moonshine can do fer yer. Yaaaaaaaaaaaaaaaarrrrrrrrrrrrrrrrn, me hearties!

Here be Freddy Scurvy. Freshly hung fer a life o' crime on the high seas. He'd sell his toothless old grandma for a mug full o' moonshine. I'd not buy her, though. She smells like ol' cabbage.

Here be poor ol' Purple Peg-leg Pete. There be tales he was hung fer a crime o' purple passion involving a peck of pickled pepper and a lass who sells sea shells on the seashore.

Here be wot remains of Crazy Cap'n Skelebones. The immortal pirate soul be dancin' the hornpipe with Davy Jones deep below the waves. He always were a fine dancer.

Blasted Bilge Mice: Master Edam Dreg
an' that swashbucklin' Rancid Red-eye Monteray Jack.

The black-hearted Captain Cheesebeard.
Never has a pirate been more feared
than he.

Why, he once battled the kraken bare-
handed with only a cocktail umbrella and
a piece of dry bread and killed 'im
stone dead.

There was calamari fer dinner fer months.

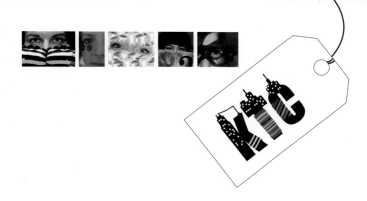

GATE OF GHOULS

Come closer, mortals... we wish to tell you a tale of terror on the London Underground.

'Tis All Hallows' Eve: the night when stitched spooks steal through the shadows.

HUSH! Did you hear that noise? From the rust-ravaged gateway to the empty echoes of abandoned Aldwych Station on The Strand, something knitty this way comes...

SQUEEEEEEEEEEAK! EEEEEEEEEK!

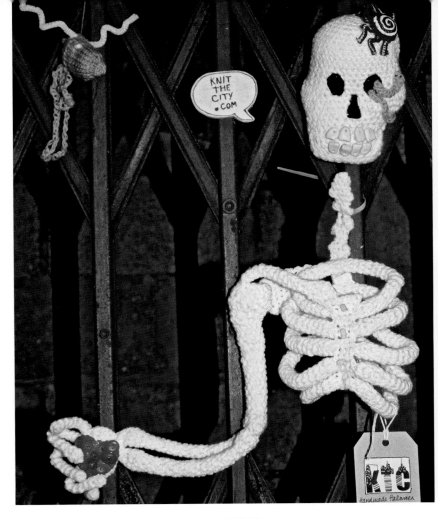

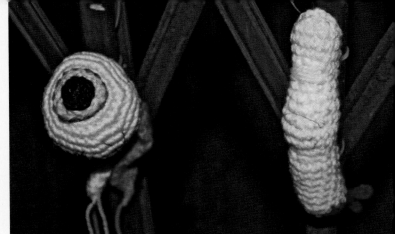

AAAIIIIEEEEE! WOOOOOOO! BLEURGH!

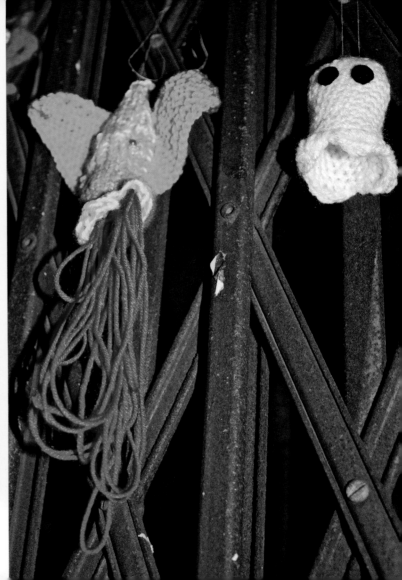

AAAAAAAAAAAAAAAAACK! OOOOOOOOOOOOOO!

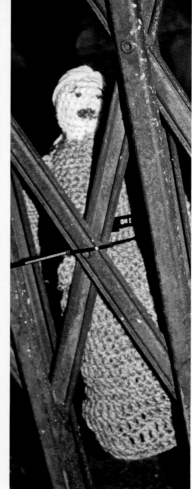

SQUEAKYSQUEAKYSQUEAKY! WAAAAAAAH! NOOOOOOOOOOOOOOOOOOOOOOOOOOOOOO!

MWA HA HA HA HAAAAAAAAAAAAAAAAAAAAAAAAAAAAAAAAAAAAAAAAAA!

STITCHED SQUID
Squidius knittius
0 metres

Deadly Knitshade

STITCHED SEA LIFE ESCAPEES

We interrupt this broadcast to bring you breaking news from London's Natural History Museum. Reports are flooding in that three of the museum's inmates have broken out of their jars and are causing havoc throughout the building.

Anyone who spots the stitched sea life escapees should keep to a safe distance and alert the authorities. I repeat, do not attempt to take them down!

SLENDER SNIPE EEL
Nemichtys scolopaceus
90 - 2000 metres

Deadly Knitshade

The unwavering cheerfulness of the slippery Slender Snipe Eel, sometimes known as the 'Deep Sea Duck', can lead to extreme hysteria.

Stitched Squid, *Squidius knittius,* Depth: 0 metres

The Stitched Squid is one of the fiercest finger-wrestlers known to man. Do not enter into combat with him. You will lose.

'Plarchie' Giant Stitched Squid, *Squidius knittius giganticus plasticus,* Depth: 1,000 metres

The group's ringleader, Plarchie the Giant Stitched Squid, has been profiled as one of the slipperiest customers of the deep sea. How many vessels this handmade horror of ten tentacled terror has taken down is impossible to calculate.

There are breaking news reports that the colossal crafty cephalopod has taken a hostage and is referring to any potential rescuers as 'puny human sushi'. His demands at this time are unclear. The advice being given is to remain calm and make no sudden moves. Experts say that eventually the squid will move on.

Eventually.

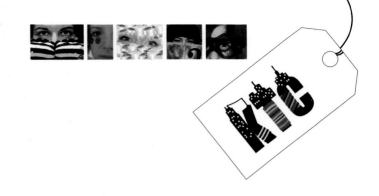

NUTCRACKER KNITMARE BEFORE CHRISTMAS

Settle in, pour a generous glug of hot mulled wine and sip from your spice-steamy mugs as we spin for you a festive fibre-filled flurry of a yarnstorming tale.

Let our Christmas dance of sneaky stitchery begin.

'Twas the Knit before Christmas in cold London Town,
Where a lone ballerina was cast with a frown,
Yet the girl was not long for her knitless despair,
For KTC's Yarn Corps soon would be there…

From out of the shadows the five stitchers came,
While visions of yarnstormings danced in their brains,
In their hands they clutched creatures of crochet and yarn,
Who hatched plans of capture and fibre-based harm.

Around the cold dancer arose such a clatter,
As small creatures stormed her and threw yarn ropes at her,
The Nutcracker Prince scaled her head in a flash,
Mouse King tickled her nose like a rodent moustache.

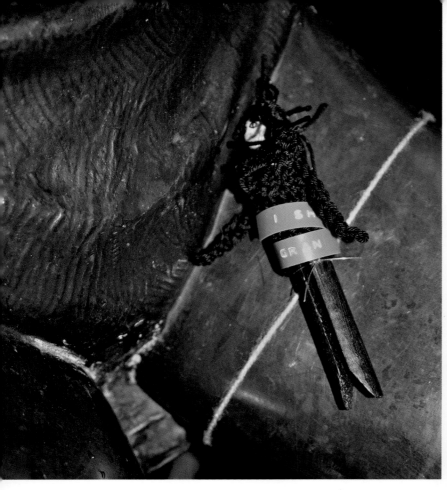

The buffoon, Russell B, chose to lurk somewhere warm,
And well-trained peg soldiers conducted a storm,

Far-too-happy flowers became creepers and flingers,
And a sour-faced snowflake was caught 'tween her fingers.

The Sugarplum Fairy, so lively and quick,
Hopped past peg doll Clara, a mere blonde-haired stick,
To climb to the shoulder and stare a red stare,
While an angry mouse soldier waved spears at her hair.

'Now, Purple! Now, Daisy! Now, Scarlet and Yellow!
Fly Lilac! Go Blue!' was the Flower's war-cry bellow
To the knobs of her knees! To the top of her bonce!
While the ruffle-dressed Spaniards climbed ropes as they danced.

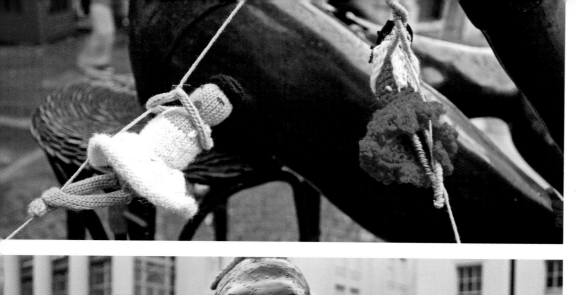

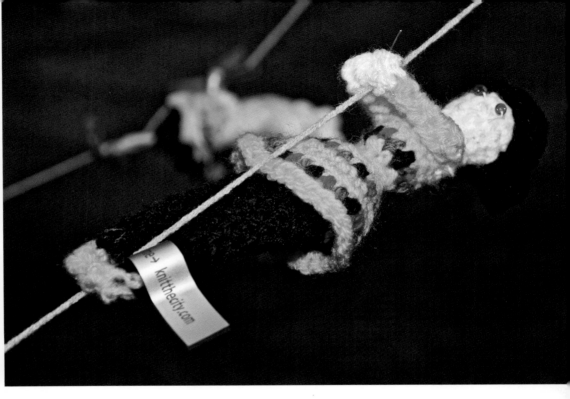

Columbine rose with her Harlequin beau,
Intent on such evil it's best not to know,
Upside down and beclawed Drosselmeyer hung to hoot,
On her knee a mouse soldier sharp-speared but quite cute.

And then, in a twinkling, the yarnstorm was done,
Frozen fingers returned to the gloves whence they'd come,
A scattering of yarn ends, a few twists of thread,
The dull ballerina was draped in stitched dread.

They spoke not a word, as they turned from their art,
Only grinned at their yarnstorm and chose to depart
But I heard them exclaim, ere they snuck out of sight,
'Scary Stitchmas to all, and to all a good-night!'

HANDMADE HERD

Ladies and gentlemen! Ewes and rams! Roll up! Roll up! Today, for one day only, those wool-slinging wonders of the Knit the City Yarn Corps will be driving a handmade herd across London Bridge before your very eyes!

We've got freakishly huge sheep! We've got horribly hungry sheep! We've got exotic spicy sheep from distant lands! We've got sheep that might not even be sheep at all! Roll up! Roll up! They have to be seen with your own eyes to be believed!

Take your seats, one and all, and listen up! By an ancient London law, way back in the eleventh century, the freeman of London have the right to drive a herd of sheep across London Bridge. KTC may not be freemen but we're free knitters! Get ready to marvel at the mutton-flavoured majesty of THE GREATEST SHEEP ON EARTH!

Entering the ring with her sticks and string, put your paws
together for Purling Paula! (Perfection in purling!)

Wonder at the wibbly world of Wobbly Walter!
(I can't look! Where will he wobble next?)

Ooooh and ahhh at the swathe of Square Sheep! (All so alike! How do they do it?!)

Behold the tottering tininess of the miniscule
Little Baa Blue! (So tiny! So teeny! So terribly titchy!)

They eat! They chomp! They chew! The bottomless bellies
that are Hungry Hairy Harriet and her blurry buddy Big-boned
Baaarry! (The munching! The crunching! The endless lunching!)

See the scarlet splendour that is roguish Red Aran
(His fleece! So outrageously ruddy!)

Be hypnotised by the handsome looks of
Handmade Hector the Baaavellous!
(I swoon! His blue eyes are so becoming!)

Glory at the gait of the GARGANTUAN Glowing Gloria! (A sheep with the semblance of a *Star Wars* AT-AT and whose magical fleece glows in the dark ! How geekishly great!)

Peer at your peril at the badly behaved and behooved Black Sheep! (Agh! The devil in dark fleece!)

Ogle the sheer unsheared spectacle of outlandish Overgrown Oscar as he croons an Elvis tune under his chaotic coiffure! (Don't step on his blue suede hooves!)

Be entranced by the lambish loveliness of Sparkly Sheila! (Sigh…)

Cry out in consternation at the covert cunning of Wilhelm, the wool-hungry wolf in sheep's clothing! (Look out behind you, Handmade Herd! The horror!)

Once more around the ring! The Handmade Herd flashes its fantastic fleeces for the crowd! Fanfares for the fleecy fellows! (What a perfect pavement-side parade!)

Put those hands together to celebrate the woolly wonder. Cheer the outstanding ovines!

Let's hear it for the baaavellous marvel that is the Handmade Herd!

May no one ever snack on your shanks! (What big teeth that last sheep has...)

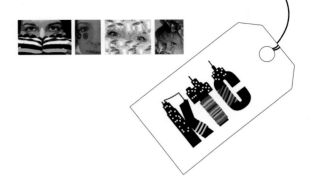

HUBBUB OF HEARTS

Love. It's squishy. It's smooshy. It's warm and cuddly. And on this day it's made from wool.

In honour of the day of mushy love that is Valentine's Day, the Knit the City Yarn Corps brought a world of woolly, yarnstorming love to the people of Piccadilly Circus.

A hubbub of hearts was wound around the Shaftesbury Memorial Fountain in the beating, buzzing heart of the city that makes our hearts skip a beat.

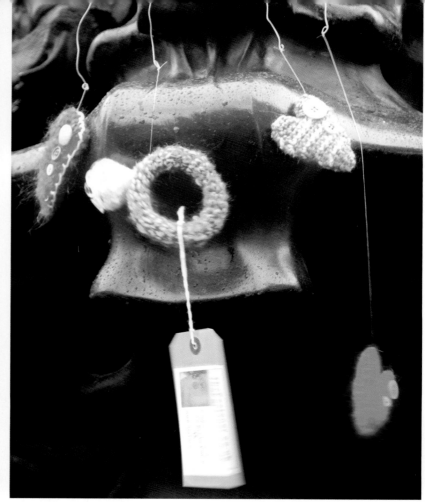

Wool you? Popping the question with buttony love...   ... squishy bling...

... a woolly Wills and Kate, and a waterfall of the web's hearty royal wedding fever.

Crafty cherubs: Anteros (the suave god of 'earthly love' and the god at the top of the Shaftesbury Memorial Fountain) and sneaky cheeky Eros (the flirty god of 'heavenly love'). Deity dignity restored with felt fig leaves.

Sealed with a stitch...

... and with a little
yarnstorming magic...

... our handmade
heartstrings grew
invisible, woolly wings
and floated above the
city to settle on the end
of the statue's bow.

Handmade mischief well
and truly managed.

With wool-wrapped love,
KTC xx

FINGER-FIGHTING STITCHED SQUID PATTERN

The Stitched Squid *(Squidius knittius)* seems a simple creature and this easy-peasy pattern takes you from square to squid quicker than a jellyfish sliding across the wet deck of a pirate ship.

Mind you watch out for his finger-wrestling ways. Ye have been warned, ye scurvy sea dogs...

Materials

- Yarn: 25 g DK acrylic yarn in a squid colour
- 4.5 mm knitting needles
- 2 x 3.5 mm double-pointed needles (DPNs)
- Scissors
- Tapestry needle
- Googly eyes
- Glue (optional if eyes aren't sticky)
- Pirate peg-leg, scurvy moustache and eyepatch to wear while making (optional)

Size

Teeny, tiny squid size, or 10 cm from head to tentacle tips.

Skills required

Knitting, i-cord, very basic, anyone-can-do-it sewing skills, and squid wrestling.

Squid head

1. Cast on 15 stitches on 4.5 mm knitting needles.
2. Knit 15 rows.
3. Cut yarn, leaving a tail about 15 cm long.
4. Using your tapestry needle, thread the yarn through all the stitches and pull to draw the stitches together.

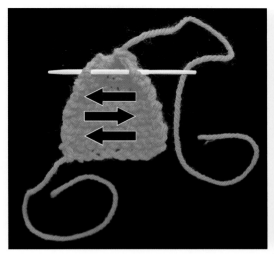

How to knit i-cord

- Cast on stitches on DPN.

- Push the stitches to the opposite end of the needle.

- Knit the stitches.

- Push the stitches to the opposite end of the needle.

- Knit stitches.

- Repeat to create i-cord.

5. Use yarn to sew the sides of the square together to make a dome shape for the head.

6. Turn inside out then lay out threads.

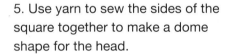

Big tentacle x 1

1. With new yarn cast on two stitches on 3.5 mm DPNs.
2. Using i-cord technique (see text box) knit 25 rows.
3. Tighten the knots at each end and carefully cut off the yarn just after the knot. Keep the cut yarn for later.

Small tentacles x 4

1. With new yarn, cast on one stitch on 3.5 mm DPNs
2. Knit 20 rows to make a long, thin tentacle.
3. Tighten the knots at each end, then carefully cut off the yarn just after the knot. Keep the cut yarn for later.

Finishing

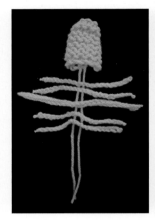

1. Lay all 5 tentacles across the yarn.

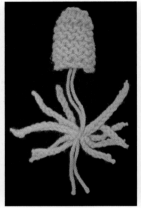

2. Tie the yarn around the tentacles and gather them together.

3. Use all cut-off yarn ends to stuff the head, then push the tentacles up.

4. Sew the tentacles in place at the back of the head.

Your squid lives!

- Stick on the googly eyes.
- Look deep into those googly eyes.
- Name your squid.
- Challenge your squid to a human vs squid battle.

Pop squid onto your fingertip for that 'Aaarrghh! He's eating me alive!' look.

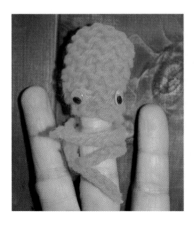

SQUARE SHEEP

The Square Sheep is a simple but baaaavellous beast, made from only a knitted square, a scrap of waste material or felt, a bit of sewing-up magic and a pair of googly eyes. He should be yarnstormed somewhere near greenery or he'll get hungry.

Materials

- Yarn: 15 g DK acrylic yarn in any colour
- 4.5 mm knitting needles
- Scrap fabric or felt
- Scissors
- Tapestry needle
- Googly eyes
- Glue (optional if eyes aren't sticky)
- Shepherd's outfit and wily sheepdog to keep your ovine in line (optional)

Size

Teeny, tiny square sheep size or 7 cm.

Skills required

Knitting, very basic, anyone-can-do-it sewing-up, cutting out, sheep-herding and wolf vigilance.

Sheep body

The main body of the sheep is formed of a simple square. The rest of the journey from square to sheep is all in the stitching-up.

1. Cast on 10 stitches in a sheepy colour of your choice.
2. Knit 15 rows.
3. Cut yarn, leaving a tail about 15 cm long.
4. Using a tapestry needle, pull the yarn through all the stitches.

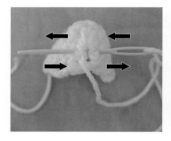     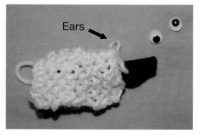

5. Use yarn to sew the ends of the square together to make the rump of the sheep.

6. Use yarn to make the loop of the tail, then tie a knot and trim.

7. Cut out a piece of fabric the same size as the body. One end should be flat, and the other should be round.

8. Lay the fabric piece inside the body with the round end poking out the opposite end to the tail.

9. Use the yarn to make two loops for ears and then tie in a knot and trim.

10. Sew the head end together as much as you can, trapping the fabric in the gap at the top to secure the head.

11. Stick on the googly eyes. Go on, it's the best bit.

Your Square Sheep lives!

Square Sheep tips

- Your square sheep doesn't have to be white: punk him up with a bit of colour.
- Hide sweets, chocolates or cursed magic rings under your sheep to keep them from sneaky thieves.
- Tuck a bouncy ball inside you sheep for that 'spring lamb' effect.
- Cram a muslin sachet of cinnamon, dried orange peel, lavender or cedar wood chips into the innards of your sheep and lock him in with your precious knitwear as a natural moth security guard.
- Do not attempt to enter into a staring contest with your sheep. Ewe will lose baaaaadly.

Warning: keep an eye out for wool-hungry wolves. They're wily fellows.

THE YARN CORPS

Operating from a secret underground wool-lined bunker in the heart of the busy metropolis of London, Knit the City's Yarn Corps spend most of their lives operating under assumed names and living like everyday people. You could sit next to one of them on the Tube, spill your pint on one of them in a crowded bar or inadvertently 'pavement dance' with them on the busy Tottenham Court Road. You would never know they were sneaky stitchers.

Four members of the original Yarn Corps are still active yarnstormers at the time of writing. Two have hung up their yarnstorming hats, and one is mysteriously missing in action.

Here are the scant details found so far...

Deadly Knitshade

One fateful night, mild-mannered Miss X (name changed to protect her identity) fell asleep while knitting on a Tube train and turned to the dark side of the Knit. She barely escaped the dreaded 'Tube sanitiser', a green, glowing, transport-cleaning monster, with her life. Details of how she survived are unclear, but there are rumours involving the rarely seen 'Tube mice' that dwell in London's subterranean transport system tunnels.

Since that night, part of her emerged from the underground as Deadly Knitshade.

Deadly Knitshade is a lone, wool-hungry wolf, instilled with eerie knitting powers. She is subject to constant unexpected 'knitblasts', leaving woolly debris around the city. It is her yarn-flavoured burden to bear. Her knits aren't content with lurking in the shadows of conventional knitting. They don't stand under the woolly umbrella of quiet stitching at home in front of the TV. They don't smell of mothballs or Werther's Originals, and they don't hide in department store basements or charity shop bargain bins. They aren't there to keep anyone warm in the winter, either.

Discernible by their Whodunnknit tags, her knitblasts can appear anywhere and everywhere. They like to get out. They demand to be noticed. They live in this city every bit as much as anyone else does.

Deadly Knitshade founded Knit the City in April 2009 and has been documenting the group's yarnstorming story, as well as her own, through her camera-wielding and word-weaving ever since. She is known for her 4 a.m. panic-stitching, her pangs of guilt at abandoning her handmade creatures and her plans to one day take over the world with an army of stitched squid.

www.whodunnknit.com

Lady Loop

Tired of a life of corsets, croquet and gaudy high society, Lady Loop fled the confines of the English gentry by thumbing her way down the M1 with a lorry driver named Jonny.

Once in London town she got hooked on yarn in the capital's gritty underground knitting bars. She now feeds her habit by hitch-hiking back to the English countryside and siphoning wool from rare-breed sheep that graze on private estates.

By day she spins the filched fleece into beautiful yarns, by night she knits it up and roams the streets looking for places to show off her ill-gotten knitted wares.

A member of KTC since the group's first outing, Lady Loop is a Jane of all crafts. Often yarnstorming in shades, she adds an unintentional air of rock-star glamour to the sneaky stitching crew. She also possesses an almost production-line craft prowess and can churn out a frightening amount of sneaky stitching pieces in one sitting.

www.ladyloop.wordpress.com

Shorn-a the Dead

A mutant hybrid of woolly Wales and New Zealand, land of the ovine zombies, Shorn-a was high on sheep dip one clear winter's night when Nelson's Column visited her in a dream and told her it was a bit chilly.

Ever since that moment, she has been on a quest to clothe London's public statuary, one legwarmer at a time. Her weapon of choice is a tasty possum-merino blend. She is something of an expert at celebrity stitching and can clone anyone in yarn.

An original member of KTC, Shorn-a is a hopeless handmade romantic, the cautious conscience of the sneaky stitching crew, and a mastermind of London's secret stories. She is prey to a deep-seated fear of moths and believes she will one day meet her end to the beat of their dusty wings.

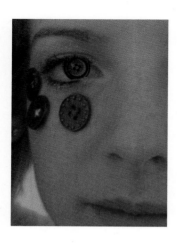

The Fastener

Banished to faraway shores for undisclosed crimes this crafty lass spent her time in exile, forced to create wonders using only found objects and mysterious purchases from the local yarn stores.

On opening a mysterious box of fastenings in a dimly lit back-alley shop, The Fastener was transformed as the contents – zips, buttons and embellishments – flew from the cursed container and stuck to her skin.

On returning home she continued her quest to clear her conscience, using her lightning-fast knitting powers to spread woolly joy wherever she roams.

Starting out with some awesome solo yarnstorming, The Fastener so impressed the Yarn Corps with her sneaky stitching skills that she was invited to join the collective in October 2009. A true stitch sage, she is known to wrangle both hook and needles like a master, and is the fastest glue gunslinger in the West. She also owns more buttons than is healthy.

www.thefastener.co.uk

Knitting Ninja

Abducted by warrior monks as a wandering street urchin, Knitting Ninja was trained to become one of the world's most deadly assassins. On a mission through London's concrete jungle she decided that avenging crimes committed against bare landscapes was a far worthier cause.

She spells out revenge with a stroke of her needle. Defying the orders of her superiors, she now dedicates her skills to making the city a place of woolly harmony. In the face of her awesome knitting ninja skills no longer shall the city lack woolly integrity. Knitting Ninja has been missing in action since the Web of Woe but there are rumours she will return one day.

MISSING IN ACTION

The Purple Purler

RETIRED

While researching into her family history, the Purple Purler discovered that she was a distant relation of the notorious Scarlet Pimpernel.

Taking her inspiration from the exploits of her cousin, she felt it only right to free the knit from the clutches of acrylic-hoarding grannies through dastardly deeds. She left her purple yarny calling card across the city. The Purple Purler withdrew from yarnstorming activities in September 2010.

Bluestocking Stitcher

RETIRED

'"By Chryst, these Southwarke stretes bore me to de'ath, They are so fuckying drab," the nun's priest sayeth.'

While reading these scribbled lines from the original fragments of *The Canterbury Tales*, Bluestocking Stitcher realised little had changed and resolved to do something about it. She took to wandering the streets with a pocketful of flowers and butterflies, adding touches of colour to the drabness, accompanied by an internal soundtrack provided by Saint Etienne. Bluestocking Stitcher left KTC in October 2010.

Please note: the identities of the Yarn Corps are classified to protect their quest for world yarnstorming domination. Suspecting any resemblance to any person, living or dead, will possibly mean you are set upon down a dark alleyway with knitted clubs and chloroform, and wake up with part of your memory 're-knitted'.

YES, BUT WHAT'S THE POINT?

What are the underlying subversive, feminist and political aims behind your woolly street art?

Desperate for us to be waving woolly protest banners, setting yarny bras on fire and shoving little old knitting ladies into a vat of hot stitched subversion? Frustrated to see we're not battling society's horrors by knitting jumpers for homeless baby penguins with tuberculosis? What's the point of what we do, dammit?! Many folks hound us for a gritty underside to our kooky little knits. We'd like to leave them wondering but they keep asking. So we'll keep it simple.

We are unashamed to admit that we yarnstorm most simply because unleashing our squishy art on the world makes us and others happy. Put an 8-metre giant knitted squid on a statue of the father of modern biology, or a giant cosy on a phone box under the paranoid gaze of CCTV, and see how it makes you feel. Go on. We'll wait here... See?

There's a bubbling love of life behind our street art. Stony-faced and outraged art has its place, but life is also beautiful, enchanting, heart-squeezingly graceful and all kinds of weird. Consider it a stitched shove that whispers 'Wake up! The world is a mad and marvellous place and we all get to live in it.'

If we must have a mission then one thing we do hope is that our sneaky stitching encourages others to bring their city to life in ways only they can imagine. After all a city without citizens is just an empty shell of a place.

We *are* women who are very passionate about our beliefs. We *do* have strong opinions and grand ideas in the tangles of our brains. We're just not screaming them through our stitching. You'll have to listen more carefully.

Change and making the world a better place can be done with a grin instead of a grimace, a whisper instead of a bellow. What we do can alter the way people look at their world. How it alters it is up to them. That's really our point. You shouldn't need to be told what to see in our stitching. It's your mind and your world. Start thinking. We'll keep on knitting.

YARNSTORMS

Phone Box Cosy (July 2009), Parliament Square, Westminster, London

Barrier Cover (June 2009), Covent Garden, London

Whale Room Knitblast (May 2009), Natural History Museum, Kensington, London

Cosy Phone Cord (June 2009), St Bartholomew's Hospital, Smithfields, London

Knitshade Blues (June 2009), Covent Garden, London

Floral Zebra Leg (June 2009), Tate Modern, Bankside, London

Punk Polecover (June 2009), Trafalgar Square, Westminster, London

Holy Knitted Lamp post Cosy, Batman (June 2009), Derby Cathedral, Derby, Derbyshire

On Yer Bike (June 2009), New Malden, Surrey

Pink Furry Knitting Learns about Trust and Pigeons (June 2009), Jubilee Bridge, Waterloo, London

Web of Woe (August 2001), Leake Street Tunnel, Waterloo, London

Oranges and Lemons Odyssey (August 2009), St Clements, City of London, London; St Martin Orgar, City of London, London; St Sepulchre-without-Newgate, City of London, London; St Leonard Shoreditch, Shoreditch, London; St Dunstans, Stepney, London; St Mary le Bow, City of London, London

Wall of Wonderland (March 2010), BFI IMAX, South Bank, London

Long Night of the Stitched Sheep (September 2010), Guildhall, City of London; Channel 4 Building, Westminster; Royal Geographical Society, Kensington; Maggie's Cancer Caring Centre, Hammersmith; Serpentine Gallery, Kensington; Royal Society of Medicine, West End; Royal Institute of British Architects, Westminster; Horse Guards, Westminster, London

Plunder of Pirates (May 2010), Pirate Castle, Camden, London

Gate of Ghouls (October 2009), Aldwych Underground Station, The Strand, London

Stitched Sea Life Escapees (August 2010), Natural History Museum, Kensington, London

Nutcracker Knitmare Before Christmas (December 2009), Enzo Plazzotta's Young Dancer Statue, Royal Opera House, Covent Garden, London

Handmade Herd (October 2011), London Bridge, London

Hubbub of Hearts (February 2011), Shaftesbury Memorial Fountain, Piccadilly Circus, London

ACKNOWLEDGEMENTS

Deadly Knitshade would like to extend her yarn-wrapped thanks to the following: Anna Martin, Hamish (who patiently put up with my constant picture-cropping pointers) and everyone at Summersdale for bringing my book home; the ever-smiling Ulla Mothes and Susanne Elste for making the first German edition of KTC so much fun; Daniella Schlingmann for first contact and coffee; my agent Carol MacArthur (floats like a butterfly, stings like a bee); Zoe and Evie of Alt Artist (camera-wrangling visionaries); Alex 'Knitterbird' Lawson, Lodvina, Laura and the good folks at the Natural History Museum; the late, great Alan 'Pottytime' Potter and his mum, June, for the yarn mountain that made our phone box; Willster for background TV appearances and booze; BNM for cycling to the station; Mr Tea for endless knittiti ideas; Sarah and Ellen (of Fleece Station fame) for bubble tea, brilliance and bad singing as I worked; Julia Goolia for Sydney-side cheerleading and knowing all along; Duke, Stephen, Paul/Chuck, and Hannah for standing in the Berlin cold; the people of Twitter and our online fans for piles of kind words; Maddy Costa for her stitched sheep; Plarchie for not eating me; the Knitshades: Mother of Poirl (4 a.m. phone box crocheter), Mole, Neh, Max and Judy for supportive insults; my fellow yarnstorming Yarn Corps past and present for pear cider and panic-knitting; Professor Lister and the nurses and staff on Bodley Scott at Bart's Hospital (Sam most of all); Amy, Perri, Joelle and Emma for the best friendship and more fun fibre-flinging than I can possibly thank you for; and most of all Gary, my long-suffering lovely sheepsketcher for carrying, cajoling and countless cups of tea.

Other people's patterns:
Love Bug by Heliinä Swerdlyk, Colourful Bug by Annukka, Crochet Frog by Armina Parnagian, Death of Rats by Hanneke Sieben, White Totoro by LucyRavenscar (find them all on www.ravelry.com).

www.knitthecity.com

www.whodunnknit.com

Follow Knit the City on Twitter: **@knitthecity**

Watch Alt Artist's Knit the City documentary videos: **www.altartist.com**

Maggie's Centre Charity (supported via Long Night of the Stitched Sheep): **www.maggiescentres.org**

www.summersdale.com

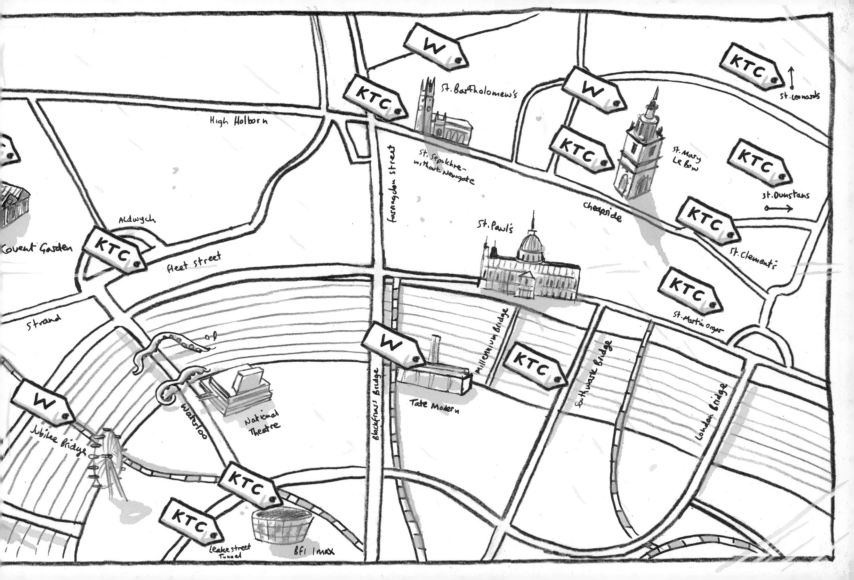

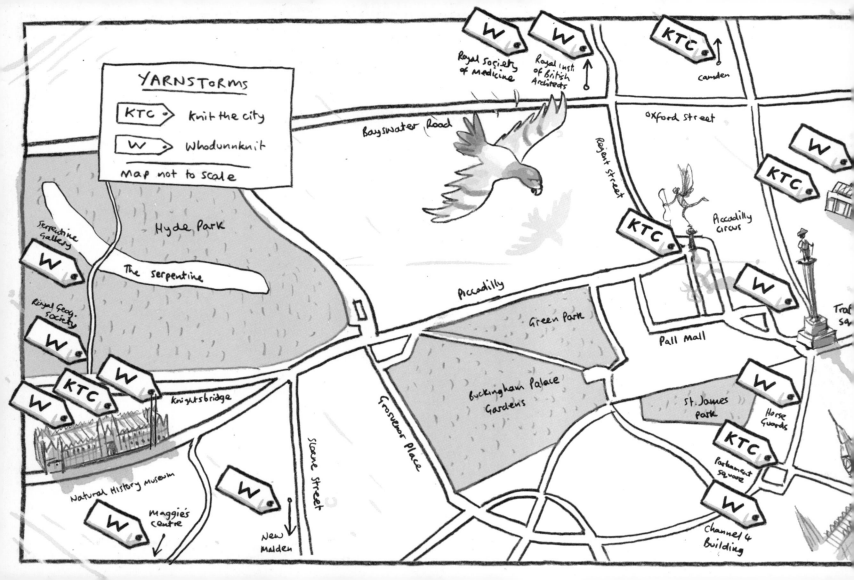